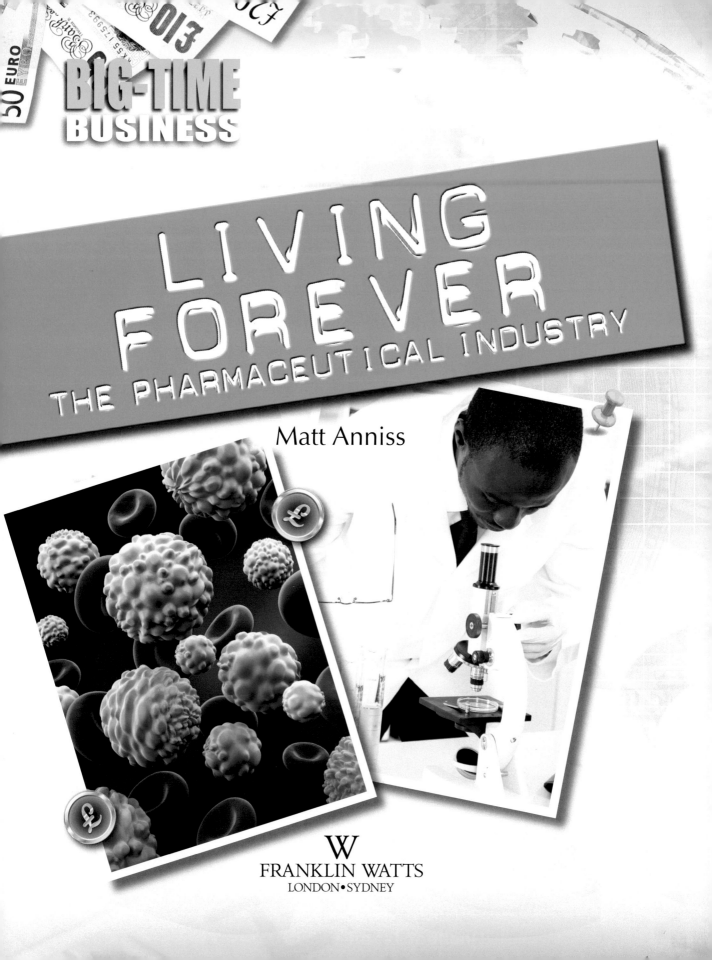

# BIG-TIME BUSINESS

# LIVING FOREVER
## THE PHARMACEUTICAL INDUSTRY

Matt Anniss

**W**
## FRANKLIN WATTS
### LONDON•SYDNEY

First published in 2015 by Franklin Watts
338 Euston Road
London NW1 3BH

Franklin Watts Australia
Level 17/207 Kent Street
Sydney, NSW 2000

Produced by Calcium

A CIP catalogue record for this book is available from
the British Library.

ISBN 978 1 4451 3917 3

Dewey classification: 338.4'76151

Printed in China

Franklin Watts is a division of Hachette Children's Books,
an Hachette UK company
www.hachette.co.uk

**Acknowledgements:**
The publisher would like to thank the following for permission to reproduce
photographs: Cover: Shutterstock: Kayros Studio l, Nenov Brothers Photography r.
Inside: Dreamstime: Alexskopje 36bl, Radu Razvan Gheorghe 41b, Huating 10tr,
Samrar35 27t, Tbe 21cl; Istockphoto: Ana Abejon 31t, Nazvin Alexey 17br, Darren
Baker 5tr, Michele Galli 34, Jodi Jacobson 16bc, Kali9 44tr, Mangostock 4–5, Monkey
Business Images 42b, Neustockimages 18bl Baris Simsek 1l, 25tr, Roel Smart 8br,
YinYang 23t; David Jordan 33cl; National Library of Medicine: 9t; Shutterstock:
Anyaivanova 13b, Yuri Arcurs 11t, 25bl, 28br, 35tr, Roxana Bashyrova 3cr, Diego Cervo
30cl, P Cruciatti 6bl, Ermek 22b, Martin Good 7b, Iofoto 19b, Michael Jung 1r, Ragne
Kabanova 14r, Kheng Guan Toh 40bl, Robert Kneschke 43tr, Dmitry Lobanov 39t, Rob
Marmion 38br, Mikeledray 16–17, Monkey Business Images 26b, Nico Tucol 20–21,
Picsfive 29b, Poznyakov 45tr, AISPIX by Image Source 32b, Thefinalmiracle 37l, Ints
Vikmanis 16br, Vovan 44br, Wavebreakmedia ltd 15b; Wikipedia: 12bl.

Every attempt has been made to clear copyright. Should there be any inadvertent
omission please apply to the publisher for rectification.

# CONTENTS

# MEDICINES WITHOUT FRONTIERS

**We have all been given medicines that have helped us get well when we have been ill.** Have you ever wondered, though, who discovered, developed and manufactured these amazing cures? The answer is the pharmaceutical industry.

## The medicine business

The pharmaceutical industry makes money by manufacturing and selling medicines. People get ill all the time so there is a huge demand for their products. In 2008 alone, the world's top 20 pharmaceutical corporations sold more than £294 million worth of drugs. One leading company, Pfizer, announced profits of more than £4.7 billion. The business of medicine makes a great deal of money.

**Every time a person goes to a pharmacy to buy medicines, he or she is helping the pharmaceutical industry to grow.**

4

## A healthy future

Making medicines is a complicated task. It can take many years to produce a new drug and prove that it is safe to use. The industry employs about 1.5 million people worldwide, and that figure is set to rise. As we all live longer, the need for medicines will increase. The pharmaceutical industry will be announcing record profits for years to come.

**Scientists in China and India are helping drug companies to make huge profits in developing countries.**

## FUTURE FACT

China accounts for 20% of the world's population but only 1.5% of the global medicine market. As the Chinese population becomes increasingly wealthier their demand for medicines will rise in future.

# CHAPTER 1

# RISE OF THE PHARMACEUTICAL INDUSTRY

**Is the pharmaceutical industry a modern invention?** Not at all! The business can trace its roots back to medieval times. The world's very first pharmacy opened in Baghdad, Iraq, more than 1,200 years ago, in 774.

## Natural remedies

In the Middle Ages there were very few tried and tested medicines. Cures offered by pharmacies tended to be potions or powders made from natural ingredients. Medieval pharmacists would grind, heat and mix leaves, plant roots and fungi to create their natural medicines.

**In some countries, such as China, traditional cures that were first developed centuries ago are still popular today.**

## The first medicine factories

The modern pharmaceutical industry began to take shape in the nineteenth century. Thanks to an increased understanding of how the human body works and new scientific methods, pharmacies in Europe and the United States were able to offer proven cures for common illnesses. It was not long before some enterprising pharmacy shop owners started opening factories to make their medicines and sell them to other pharmacy shops.

# PHARMACY ROOTS

Many big pharmaceutical corporations can trace their roots back to nineteenth century pharmacy shops. Boots started life in the mid-nineteenth century when its founder, John Boot, opened a small herbalist shop in Nottingham to treat local patients. The business is today worth billions of pounds.

**Today, Boots is one of the leading chemists in the UK pharmaceutical industry.**

# MEDICAL WONDERS

**In the early 1900s many new medicines were discovered and the industry quickly grew.** Companies such as Merck (MSD), which perfected a method of producing penicillin on an enormous scale, began to spend more money on researching new cures. As a result, drugs such as aspirin, paracetamol and insulin were all introduced.

## Safety issues

By the 1950s and 1960s, the pharmaceutical industry was booming. Fuelled by great scientific breakthroughs and more accurate methods, a wave of new 'wonder drugs' were introduced. Not all of the new drugs were safe, however, and the pharmaceutical industry was rocked by scandals.

**Aspirin is now a familiar cure for a variety of conditions, but when it was first developed it was thought of as a medical miracle.**

The work of many brilliant scientists, such as Alexander Flemming, during the twentieth century led to the development of a number of life-saving drugs.

## DEADLY DRUG

The biggest medical scandal of the 1960s involved the drug Thalidomide, which was given to pregnant women suffering from morning sickness. In 1961, sales were stopped when scientists discovered that thousands of women in Europe who had taken the drug had given birth to babies with severe disabilities. Tragically, many of these babies died.

## Testing is enforced

In 1964, the World Medical Association introduced laws that forced pharmaceutical companies to test drugs more thoroughly. Before new drugs could go on sale, the companies that made them had to prove that the drugs had been carefully tested and were safe for the public to use.

# CHAPTER 2

# MAKING MEDICINES

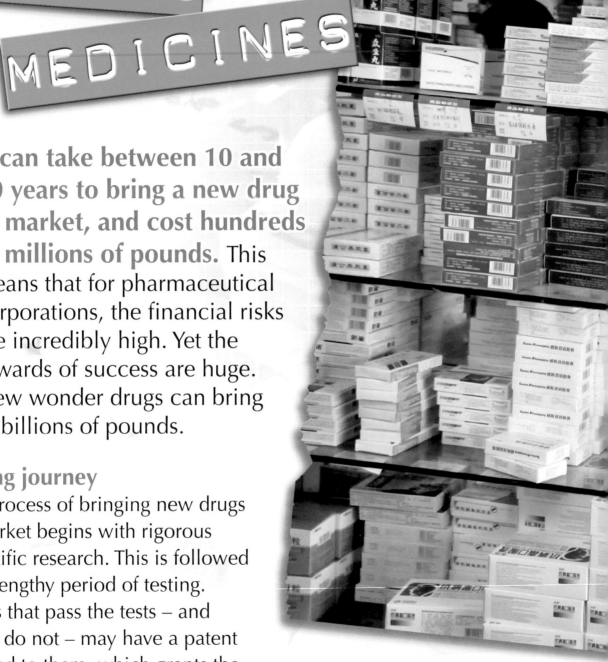

**It can take between 10 and 20 years to bring a new drug to market, and cost hundreds of millions of pounds.** This means that for pharmaceutical corporations, the financial risks are incredibly high. Yet the rewards of success are huge. New wonder drugs can bring in billions of pounds.

## A long journey

The process of bringing new drugs to market begins with rigorous scientific research. This is followed by a lengthy period of testing. Drugs that pass the tests – and many do not – may have a patent applied to them, which grants the pharmaceutical corporation exclusive sales' rights for a number of years.

**Each of the drugs on these shelves could have taken up to 15 years to devise and develop.**

The pills being given to this patient may have been made in China or India, before being shipped back to Europe.

## Manufactured in Asia

Once a new drug has been granted a patent, it can be manufactured. Many medicines developed in Europe and the United States are made in factories in China and India, where production costs are far lower. The drugs are then shipped back to the West, where the process of selling them to health maintenance organisations (HMOs), hospitals and pharmacies begins.

**FUTURE FACT**

It is estimated that the global pharmaceutical industry is currently worth around £62 billion. Year on year the industry is growing by an average of five per cent. That means in 10 years time the industry could be worth £100 billion.

# RESEARCH AND DEVELOPMENT

**All around the world, scientists in laboratories are busy working on research to find new drugs.** Many are employed by universities and colleges. Others work directly for pharmaceutical companies.

## Investing in research

One area of research that pharmaceutical companies invest in heavily is dangerous diseases such as cancer. They hope that their scientists will be able to identify new chemical compounds that have the potential to fight, control or cure illnesses.

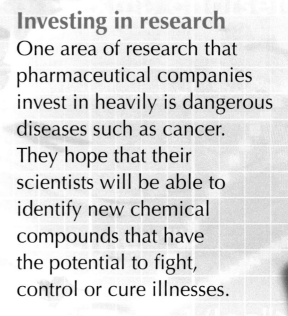

**The research of brilliant US scientist John Craig Venter has been the basis of many important medical discoveries in the field of genetically inherited disease.**

**It can take years of work in laboratories such as this one to create a new drug.**

## Drug discovery

Scientists may spend years trying thousands of different chemical combinations before they find a formula for a successful drug. Only 1 in 25 successful formulas for medicines will go on to be tested on humans and by this point the pharmaceutical company will already have spent many millions of pounds.

## STEM CELL RESEARCH

Pharmaceutical companies are spending many millions of pounds on stem cell research. Stem cells are the 'building block' cells of our bodies. They have the potential to become any type of cell in the body. Stem cells can become cells of the blood, heart, bones, skin, muscles and the brain. They can also renew and multiply themselves. Scientists clone stem cells from an existing human body and alter the cells to help cure a particular illness.

# CLINICAL TRIALS

**Once a new drug has been discovered, it must be tested.** First, 'test tube studies' are conducted in the laboratory, where scientists can carefully monitor just how the drug affects human body cells. If the results are positive, the drug may then be tested on animals and then on humans.

## Testing drugs on humans

Tests in which drugs are tried out on humans for the first time are called clinical trials. Before these tests can take place, permission must be sought from the government agencies or regulatory bodies that oversee the pharmaceutical industry.

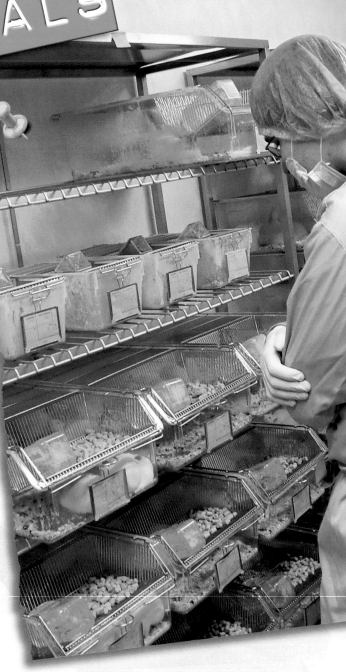

**Scientists often test new drugs on rats and mice before testing them on people.**

14

# SEEDING TRIALS

In 2001, 12 leading medical magazines ran an article accusing US pharmaceutical companies of using 'seeding trials' to sell their products. This means the companies paid doctors to give their new drugs to patients. The doctors were being paid, so they were rarely critical of the medicines, even when they should have been.

## Treating real illnesses

Clinical trials can continue for some time – often for a number of years – and involve several studies in different countries. After first testing a drug on animals, scientists then test the drug on healthy people to see how they react. If the drug is proved safe for use, it is tested on people who have the illness that the drug is designed to treat. Experts are asked to watch the trials and report on whether the new drug works.

**Physicians carefully monitor children who take part in clinical trials to make sure that new drugs are safe.**

# PATENT

## PENDING

## Exclusive sales' rights

To be able to get a patent, the pharmaceutical company must provide proof that the drug works, is safe and produces no harmful side effects. Once the company has been granted the patent, it has the right to sell the drug exclusively for a set period of time.

**If the clinical trials of a new drug are successful, the pharmaceutical company will apply for a patent for the drug.** A patent is a document that says you invented something and grants you the right to sell it for a set period, which is usually 20 years. While the application is being considered, the patent is said to be 'pending', or waiting to happen.

**To have a chance of securing a patent, pharmaceutical companies must submit a lot of detailed paperwork.**

*†Compare to the active ingredient in Advil®*

For Body Aches and Pains
**IBUPROFEN**
IBUPROFEN CAPSULES, 200mg
Pain Reliever-Fever Reducer (NSAID)
SEE NEW WARNINGS INFORMATION
80 SOFTGELS™ LIQUID FILLED CAPSULES™
Softgel

# THE COST OF PATENTS

Pharmaceutical companies develop many new drugs at the same time, but only a small number of them are granted a patent. Including research and testing, each successful drug patent costs the pharmaceutical company about £76 million.

## Hard to get

In the United States, the US Food and Drug Administration (FDA) grants patents for all new drugs. Their Center for Drug Evaluation and Research oversees the New Drug Application (NDA) process. In 2010, they approved just 21 new drugs for use. This was a tiny proportion of the applications received.

**Pharmaceuticals must sell millions of drugs in order to get a return on their investment.**

# MARKETING MEDICINES

Sales of new wonder drugs need to be huge to cover the enormous amount of money spent on research and development. So pharmaceutical companies spend vast amounts of money on marketing to boost their sales. They may spend twice the amount they spent on research.

## What is marketing?

Marketing is the process of raising people's awareness of a product so that they will buy it. Pharmaceutical companies use a number of different marketing methods to try to increase sales. They place adverts on television and in magazines, for example, and give away free samples.

**Pictures such as this one are often used in adverts for pain relief tablets.**

18

## The role of reps

Most marketing of new drugs is directed at doctors and hospital administrators, because these are the people who have the power to prescribe the drugs and place orders for them. Pharmaceutical corporations pay sales people called pharmaceutical reps (which is short for 'representatives') to talk to physicians around the country about the company's medicines.

## FUTURE FACT

In the future, the Internet will change the way pharmaceutical companies market their drugs. There are likely to be fewer pharmaceutical reps and greater use of 'e-marketing' aimed directly at HMOs, hospitals and pharmacies.

**Thousands of pharmaceutical reps work in the United Kingdom.**

# CHAPTER 3

# THE BIG PLAYERS

## Pfizer and Merck (MSD)

Two of the three biggest pharmaceutical companies in the world are based in the United States. Between them, Pfizer and Merck (MSD) employ more than 250,000 people, who help make and sell some of the world's most popular medicines.

**There are many hundreds of pharmaceutical companies worldwide, but the market is dominated by just a handful of big corporations.** These drug giants often have long histories and a proven track record of discovering, developing and delivering drugs. Because of their massive size and cash reserves, they can outmuscle smaller companies by spending more on research, development and marketing.

**The marketing and sales teams of big pharmaceutical companies work together to help drive sales of drugs.**

## Tough competition

Corporations such as Pfizer and Merck (MSD) owe some of their size to buying up smaller pharmaceutical companies. In order to compete with these giants, other medical companies around the world have joined forces. British company GlaxoSmithKline, for example, came about after two huge corporations, GlaxoWellcome and SmithKline Beecham, merged in 2000.

**FUTURE FACT**

Over the last 10 years, the number of companies making drugs has fallen. This trend is likely to continue in the future as leading corporations buy or merge with smaller companies.

German pharmaceutical company Bayer had a revenue of almost £16 billion in 2013.

# RISKY BUSINESS

**The pharmaceutical industry is seeing growing sales and profits.** Yet the business remains a risky one. Bad decisions or poor research can lead to billions of pounds being wasted. For pharmaceutical corporations, the difference between success and failure can be enormous.

## Limiting the risk

As we have seen, it takes a lot of time and money to bring a new drug to market. Although pharmaceutical companies try to protect themselves against making the wrong choices by researching and testing many new drugs at once, there are no guarantees that any of their drugs will be approved. A run of failures can harm a company's share price and future growth.

**How well a pharmaceutical company is doing will be reflected in its share price. A higher share price means bigger profits.**

7691.08

7274.08

17.27

6857.08

6.02

4.37

3.2

6440.08

**Pharmaceutical companies must carry out careful research to try to ensure a drug will sell once it makes it to market.**

## THE COST OF FAILURE

In March 2008, British pharmaceutical giant Astra Zeneca saw its share price tumble after five different new drugs, including stroke and lung cancer treatments, failed to get past the trial stage. As a result, the company was worth less than a quarter of what it had been a year earlier. Since then share prices have recovered.

## A competitive market

Even if a new drug does make it to market, it must sell in huge numbers. Drugs are often patented before trial, so by the time the drug reaches the market, companies have only five or seven years of the 20-year patent period left in which to maximise sales before competitors are allowed to make their own versions (known as generic drugs). Poor sales could lose the company hundreds of millions of pounds.

# BILLION-POUND BUSINESSES

**Sometimes a pharmaceutical company strikes gold!** It develops a wonder drug that sells in vast numbers around the world and makes the company a huge profit. The money it makes from sales of the drug far outweighs the amount it spent on researching, developing and marketing the drug.

## Stem cell cures

Stem cell research is an area that is currently receiving huge investment from pharmaceutical companies. It is hoped that the research will help create wonder drugs that can cure conditions such as Parkinson's disease, Alzheimers and diabetes.

**Stem cells, here seen through a powerful microscope, are the basis for some amazing new cures.**

# CANCER CURE

In November 2011, scientists announced that they had developed a revolutionary wonder drug that could cure many forms of cancer and save millions of lives. The drug, named 'KG5', could be approved and on sale by 2016, making its patent holders, US pharmaceutical company Amitech Therapeutic Solutions, many billions.

## The success of Prozac

US corporation Eli Lilly and Company struck gold when it launched a drug called Prozac in 1987. Prozac was heralded as a brilliant new treatment for depression. In its first year alone, it made Eli Lilly more than £200 million. Until its patent ran out in 2001, Prozac sales reached almost £2.5 billion.

## Something in the water

Antidepressants are so widely prescribed in many Western countries that traces of these drugs have been found in freshwater streams, rivers and even in drinking water.

**People who do not suffer from depression may be absorbing traces of antidepressants by drinking tap water.**

# MANAGING THE IMAGE

## Paying for good publicity

Many pharmaceutical companies pay public relations (PR) or media management companies to send positive stories about them to the media, and respond to any bad publicity. They spend hundreds of thousands of pounds each year on PR.

**Pharmaceutical corporations are not always well liked.**
Over the years, they have battled accusations about their business practices, the costs of medicines and scandals over failed drugs. Bad stories such as these can harm sales, so companies spend a lot of time and money managing their public image.

**Sometimes, new drugs are given to pregnant women that harm the development of unborn babies. Although these instances are rare today, if they do occur, the pharmaceutical industry must react quickly to prevent bad press.**

**Some companies give away millions of pounds worth of medicines to help wipe out deadly diseases.**

## Partnering charities

Many pharmaceutical corporations partner with charities and health organisations to help ill people in the developing world. Merck (MSD) has donated billions of doses of its drug Mectizan to the Carter Center to help fight river blindness in Africa. It has also donated drugs to the South African government to help stop the spread of the disease HIV/AIDS.

**FUTURE FACT**

A tropical disease called lymphatic filariasis may be wiped out completely within the next 10 years. GlaxoSmithKline and Merck (MSD) have pledged to provide free drugs until the illness is destroyed.

# CHAPTER 4
# CONTROVERSIES AND CHALLENGES

**Pharmaceutical companies are rarely ever out of the news.** As if running some of the world's biggest corporations was not difficult enough, the bosses of pharmaceutical companies often have to deal with big challenges and global controversies. With the health of sick people on the line, the stakes are rarely less than incredibly high.

**Decisions taken by pharmaceutical companies can affect the lives of millions of ill people around the world.**

## Bad news

Sometimes pharmaceutical companies must face up to the fact that people have become ill after taking new medicines. This can happen as a result of mistakes made by people within the pharmaceutical industry. Another challenge they face is having to argue with national governments about the cost of medicines. They constantly have to balance the goal of making money against the need to keep the world healthy.

## DRUG PANIC

In August 2011, the pharmaceutical company Reckitt Benkhiser was forced to recall thousands of packets of a pain relief drug called Nurofen Plus. Several batches sent to pharmacies in London were found to contain a powerful drug used in the treatment of mental health illnesses.

**In 2011, one pharmaceutical company had to remove a popular drug from sale following a health scare.**

## Is the price fair?

Giant pharmaceutical corporations develop and sell medicines in order to make money, but many people in developing countries who need their drugs cannot afford to buy them. Like a lot of other controversies and challenges that the pharmaceutical industry faces every year, this is a problem that refuses to go away.

29

# FEAR TACTICS?

In countries, such as the United States, where pharmaceutical companies are allowed to advertise their drugs directly to the consumer, the adverts can be scary. They quite often show the bad effects of a particular disease. Critics of the pharmaceutical industry say that this is a deliberate plan by companies to play up the effects of certain illnesses.

## Scare stories

According to critics, the pharmaceutical industry uses disease-mongering tactics to boost sales of its drugs and medicines. If more people think they may have picked up a certain illness, or suffer from a certain condition, they are more likely to go and see their doctor and ask him or her to prescribe something for the problem.

**Critics say that the pharmaceutical industry tries to increase sales by telling us we are sicker than we really are. They call this 'disease-mongering'.**

**Testing people for illnesses such as diabetes can help drive sales of drugs.**

## The case for the defence

The pharmaceutical industry denies that it uses disease-mongering tactics. It argues that all it does is offer information to the public about illnesses and the drugs that could help fight or cure them. It also points out that it has no control over what medicines doctors actually prescribe for their patients.

# THE COST OF ERROR

Most new drugs developed and sold by pharmaceutical companies are safe. A small number, however, prove to have unpredicted side effects. On occasion, drugs that may help treat one illness are found to cause other health problems. When this happens, it can cost the pharmaceutical corporation billions of pounds.

If people become ill after taking a drug, it is bad news for the pharmaceutical industry.

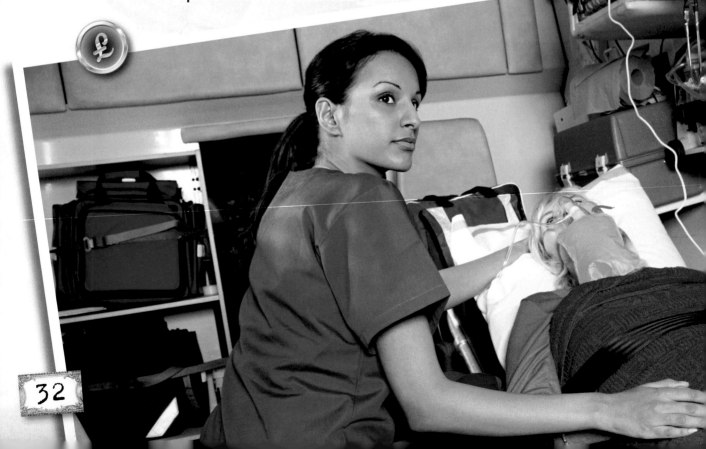

## Initial success ...

When Merck (MSD) launched Vioxx in 1999, it was marketed as a wonder drug that would relieve the pain of many millions of arthritis sufferers. It was a huge success and by 2003, sales had risen to more than £1.47 billion a year.

## MARKETING MISHAP

US pharmaceutical giant Eli Lilly was fined a record £300 million and forced to pay out billions of pounds in compensation, after being found guilty of playing down the side effects of the mental health drug Zyprexa. Thousands of people who took the drug put on weight and developed diabetes.

Complimentary • ONCE DAILY • 2 Tablets • No. 3810
VIOXX® 12.5 mg
(rofecoxib tablets)
0505500

MEDIC

**Vioxx was one of Merck (MSD)'s best-selling drugs until it was withdrawn.**

## Withdrawn from sale

In 2004, Merck (MSD) took the dramatic decision to withdraw Vioxx from sale because of safety concerns. The FDA estimated that Vioxx had caused between 88,000 and 139,000 heart attacks in five years. Since then, Merck (MSD) has paid out hundreds of millions of pounds in compensation to former users. Eventually, the total cost to the company could be £3 billion.

# COSY

# RELATIONSHIPS

**Researchers, doctors and pharmaceutical companies have always had a close relationship.** Some people think it is too close and that the pharmaceutical industry has too much power over health and science professionals.

**Pharmaceutical companies have been criticised for offering doctors free gifts, such as skiing holidays.**

## Tied by money

Critics say that some scientists feel under pressure to deliver the results that pharmaceutical companies want, because it is these companies that pay their wages. They allege that some scientists will design tests that deliver results that show new drugs in only a favourable light.

**Critics say scientific research used by the pharmaceutical industry is flawed.**

## New guidelines

In recent years, the relationship between pharmaceutical reps and doctors has been in the spotlight. For example, in the past, it was not uncommon for US pharmaceutical reps to offer gifts as incentives to doctors in order to get them to buy their medicines. Following criticism, the US pharmaceutical industry introduced new guidelines in 2009 to end these practices.

## NO FREE GIFTS

The close relationship between pharmaceutical reps and doctors is not just an issue in the United States. In the United Kingdom rules have been introduced to try to put an end to the free gifts given by pharmaceutical companies to doctors in order to persuade them to promote their drugs.

**Around the world, and particularly in Africa, millions of people suffer from a potentially deadly disease called HIV/AIDS.** Plenty of cutting-edge drug treatments exist to fight the disease but because pharmaceutical companies own the patents, they can charge top prices.

**It is much easier for people in the West to get the drugs they need to combat HIV/AIDS.**

## DANGEROUS DRUG TRIALS

The pharmaceutical company Pfizer was accused of testing a new, unproven drug on 100 children in Nigeria in 1996 without their permission. Several children died and others became ill. In 2009, Pfizer agreed to pay out £44 million in compensation to the victims.

**In developing countries, children with HIV/AIDS now have a chance to live thanks to donated drugs.**

## Making a stand

It costs an estimated £6,000 per person, per year to treat HIV/AIDS in South Africa, where hundreds of thousands of people have the disease. In 2001, the South African government said it could not afford to pay such high prices. The government passed a law that allowed drugs companies to bypass the patents on HIV/AIDS medicines. This meant that generic drugs could be produced and given to sufferers at a fraction of the price.

## The industry backs down

The pharmaceutical companies decided to sue the South African government. However, in the face of mounting pressure from campaigners, they eventually backed down. Now they work with the World Health Organization to offer cheap or free HIV/AIDS drugs in developing countries.

# CHAPTER 5

# FUTURE OF PHARMACEUTICALS

**One day soon, we may all be able to live for 130 years, or perhaps even longer.** This might sound far-fetched, but scientists at leading pharmaceutical companies are already working on new drugs that could help our cells (the building blocks of our bodies) to slow down the ageing process.

## Keeping ahead of the game

New research and drug creation techniques are being developed all the time. As our understanding of science and the human body increases, pharmaceutical companies will be able to produce more powerful drugs to treat many of the world's most dangerous diseases.

**Thanks to medical science, many people now live longer, healthier lives.**

People with diabetes must inject themselves with insulin to control the condition. It is hoped that pharmaceuticals will create a vaccine for Type 1 diabetes within the next 20 years.

## Challenges ahead

The pharmaceutical industry still has challenges to face, though. The debate over the balance between keeping the world healthy and maximising company profits will continue and the industry's business practices will be scrutinised more than ever.

### FUTURE FACTS

By 2035, it is estimated that diabetes will affect 10 per cent of the British population. Pharmaceutical companies are racing to create a cure for this devastating condition.

39

# AGE OF THE INTERNET

**Since the Internet boom of the 1990s, the World Wide Web has changed the way most companies do business.** The pharmaceutical industry was quick to see that by using the Internet, it could get its message across directly to potential customers.

## Online selling

As well as having their own corporate websites with information about their businesses, pharmaceutical companies also have sites for each of their branded medicines. These websites are designed not only to provide advice and safety information, but also to sell medications to pharmacies, doctors and ordinary people.

**Many people now buy their medicines through online pharmacies.**

online Medicine

## Plugging products

Websites for 'over-the-counter medicines' (ones that you can buy from a pharmacy without a prescription) either offer links to online pharmacies or talk up the benefits of the products to encourage you to buy them. For non-prescription products, the web has proved to be a very useful marketing tool.

# PHARMACY CLAMPDOWN

The UK government has recently ordered an investigation of the UK pharmaceutical industry after allegations that it has been working with pharmacies to inflate the price of some drugs.

**Many people now prefer to buy non-prescription medicines online.**

# FIGHTING ILLEGAL MEDICINES

**Numerous online pharmacies offer prescription drugs for sale direct to the public.** In the United Kingdom, many of these businesses will not sell drugs to people without a prescription from a doctor. There are, however, a lot of online businesses around the world that will.

When people consult a doctor and are given a prescription, they can discuss how to obtain the medicine safely.

## Cheap drugs

In Europe, many online pharmacies give no guarantee that the drugs they sell are safe. Buying from them is illegal and shoppers who are caught can be sent to prison. People continue to take the risk, however, because medications bought from online pharmacies are usually much cheaper.

**Buying online is risky because you cannot fully know what you are purchasing.**

## LIFESTYLE DRUGS

Many people use online pharmacies to buy so-called 'lifestyle drugs', which treat non-threatening conditions such as baldness or acne. The market for these drugs is very lucrative for the pharmaceutical industry.

## A growing problem

Europeans now spend millions each year buying drugs from foreign online pharmacies, many of which do not follow industry regulations. Not only does this pose a risk to people's health, because they may not be buying drugs from a reputable source, it also represents a significant loss of potential profits for pharmaceutical companies. It is a growing problem for health services and the pharmaceutical industry.

# LIVING FOREVER

In 1911, the average life expectancy of a person in a wealthy Western country was 47 years but in 2011 it was nearly 80! These amazing statistics show just how big a difference 100 years of medical and pharmaceutical advances have made to the way we live our lives. We are now living much longer. By 2050, the life expectancy of a Western woman could be close to 100 years.

**As people live longer in the future, the pharmaceutical industry is likely to grow even bigger.**

## Drug use set to increase

Longer life expectancy is great news for the pharmaceutical industry. As people get older, they need more drugs and medications to keep them healthy. If more of us live longer, demand for key drugs will rocket. For the pharmaceutical industry this means ever-increasing future sales.

**Amazing new drugs are helping people to live longer, healthier, more active lives.**

## FUTURE FACT

The world's population currently stands at about 7.2 billion. According to United Nations' projections, by 2050 it could have topped 10 billion. That is a lot more people for the pharmaceutical industry to keep healthy!

## New drugs offer hope

Over the next 50 years our understanding of how to treat deadly diseases will increase significantly. Pharmaceutical companies will develop new wonder drugs to fight cancer, HIV/AIDS and other deadly illnesses.

These drugs will be sold at premium prices, allowing pharmaceutical companies to announce record profits for years to come.

# GLOSSARY

**billion** 1,000 million, or 1,000,000,000

**branded medicines** drugs sold to the public and health professionals using a trade name, for example, Prozac

**cash reserves** money that companies have stored in a bank for future use

**cloning** producing an accurate copy of something, such as body cells

**compensation** money paid to a person by a company if the person has suffered because of something the company has done

**controversies** major disputes, usually held in public

**depression** a disease of the mind that makes people feel miserable

**disabilities** permanent problems with the mind or body, such as legs that are unable to work or severe mental illness

**e-marketing** electronic marketing done using email or the Internet

**exclusive** restricted to one person or company

**generic drugs** cheap copies of drugs no longer protected by a patent

**incentives** gifts given to someone to encourage them to do something specific

**laboratories** the rooms in which scientists carry out research and experiments

**mental health drug** a medicine used to treat a disease of the mind

**mental health illnesses** diseases of the mind

**patent** a legal document that proves you are the inventor of a product and makes it illegal for other people to copy your invention

**physician** another word for doctor

**premium prices** sums added to the ordinary prices of goods, making them more expensive

**prescription drugs** drugs for which you need a doctor's prescription or note to buy

**profits** money that a business makes on top of the money it has spent on buying or producing something

**public relations** the business of managing the public image of a company or individual

**research** finding out more about something in order to understand it better

**share price** the price for which a company share can be bought or sold. If the share price is high, the company is doing well.

**side effects** illnesses or physical conditions that result from taking a particular medicine

**successful formulas** combinations of chemicals proven to work as medicines

**sue** to take somebody to court over something they have said or done

**suicidal thoughts** thinking about killing yourself

# FOR MORE INFORMATION

## BOOKS

*Finding Better Medicines* (Why Science Matters), John Coad, Heinemann Library

*Health and Medicines: The Impact of Science and Technology* (Pros and Cons), Anne Rooney, Gareth Stevens

*The Pharmaceutical Industry* (Global Industries Uncovered), Richard Spilsbury, Wayland

*The Story of Medicine*, Anne Rooney, Arcturus

## WEBSITES

Find out more about the pharmaceutical industry and your health at:

www.fda.gov

www.gsk.com

www.kidshealth.org/teen/index.jsp?tracking=T_Home

www.nhs.uk

**Note to parents and teachers**
Every effort has been made by the Publisher to ensure that these websites contain no inappropriate or offensive material. However, because of the nature of the Internet, it is impossible to guarantee that the contents of these sites will not be altered. We strongly advise that Internet access is supervised by a responsible adult.

# INDEX